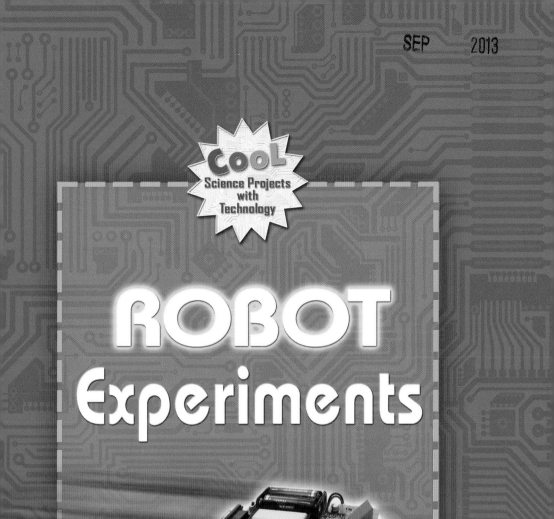

Cool
Science Projects
with
Technology

ROBOT
Experiments

Ed Sobey, PhD

Enslow Publishers, Inc.
40 Industrial Road
Box 398
Berkeley Heights, NJ 07922
USA

http://www.enslow.com

To Professor Ken Vickers at the University of Arkansas,
who is always an inspiration and instigator

Acknowledgements

I thank Parallax, Inc., who sent me a robot kit many years ago. Thanks to
PICAXE and their U.S. distributor Advanced Micro Circuits, run by Dr. Andrew
Veronis. Fred Martin, Assistant Professor of Computer Science at the University
of Massachusetts, Lowell, helped with computer software and sent me a
Super Cricket (sold by Gleason Research) to test. Thanks to Susan Johnson and
Bellevue Community College for supplying one of the photos in this book.

Library of Congress Cataloging-in-Publication Data

Sobey, Edwin J. C., 1948–
    Robot experiments / Ed Sobey.
        p. cm. — (Cool science projects with technology)
    Includes bibliographical references and index.
     Summary: "Presents several science projects dealing with robots"—Provided by
publisher.
     ISBN 978-0-7660-3303-0
     1. Robotics—Juvenile literature. 2. Robots—Design and construction—Juvenile
literature. I. Title.
    TJ211.2.S63 2011
    629.8'92—dc22   2009037897

Printed in the United States of America

092010 Lake Book Manufacturing, Inc., Melrose Park, IL

10 9 8 7 6 5 4 3 2 1

To Our Readers: We have done our best to make sure all Internet Addresses in this
book were active and appropriate when we went to press. However, the author and
the publisher have no control over and assume no liability for the material available
on those Internet sites or on other Web sites they may link to. Any comments or
suggestions can be sent by e-mail to comments@enslow.com or to the address on the
back cover.

♻ Enslow Publishers, Inc., is committed to printing our books on recycled paper. The
paper in every book contains 10% to 30% post-consumer waste (PCW). The cover board
on the outside of each book contains 100% PCW. Our goal is to do our part to help
young people and the environment too!

Photo Credits: All photos by Ed Sobey, except Shutterstock, p. 7; Susan Johnson, pp. 21,
54.

Cover Photo: © iStockphoto.com; Ed Sobey (robot).

Contents

R0429201407

Experiments with a ♦ symbol feature Ideas for a Science Fair Project.

Experiments with a ❀ symbol feature Ideas for a Science Fair Project.

What Are Robots? An Introduction

Have you ever wished you had a robot to clean your room for you, or even do your homework? Perhaps you've seen *Star Wars* or other science fiction films in which robots display artificial intelligence. There are already cars that can parallel park by themselves—but are they real robots? Can an everyday person build one?

There are several ways to define *robot*, but most people agree that a robot is a machine that can act without human direction. That is, once started, it can perform useful work on its own without receiving further instructions from a person. Of course, your toaster and refrigerator both meet that criteria, but they are not robots. So what makes a true robot?

A robot is more than a machine acting by itself. A robot must also be programmable. Your computer fits that description: it's a machine that you can program. But we don't consider a computer a robot because it doesn't move itself or outside objects. Yes, it spins a CD or DVD, but it doesn't move anything externally.

Going back to the toaster, it moves stuff, mostly bread and bagels, and it is programmable. You can program it for "light" or "dark." But it's still not a robot. You can't reprogram the toaster to do anything except make toast.

So a robot is a machine that moves itself or other things. It can also act autonomously using a set of instructions called a program. The program can be changed to make the robot perform different tasks. Some robots can gather information from their environment and respond intelligently to that information.

This lengthy definition suggests a list of components required for making a robot:

- Movement requires a motor.

- Movement also requires wheels, treads, or legs.

- *Acting autonomously* requires an onboard computer or microprocessor.

- Detecting an environment requires sensors: light, infrared light, touch, or some other type.

- Operating the motors and the computer requires a source of power.

- Being programmable requires a way to download programs from another computer—either via cable, infrared link, or wireless link.

- Being programmable also requires a computer language that both you and the robot can understand.

Robots are machines that move and are controlled by programs written on computers.

Although robots may come from science fiction, they are becoming a daily reality. Robots are used in industry to weld parts together, spray paint parts, assemble those parts, and load materials onto pallets for shipping. In some large office buildings, robots deliver and pick up the mail from each office. Increasingly, research scientists use them to explore space and ocean depths. Artists use them to create moving sculptures. Robots are showing up in more and more homes. They perform some of the jobs that people don't like to do, such as vacuuming the floor and cutting the grass.

The Scientific Method and Science Fairs

You can run many experiments with robots, but to use these in a science fair, you need to follow some guidelines. Doing a science experiment includes making observations, measuring variables, collecting and analyzing data, researching scientific reports, and making an attractive and easy-to-understand report. Simply making a robot is not science.

Start your project by playing around with robots. This is the best way to learn. Ask yourself questions about how they operate and what they can do. As you learn more, ask better and more detailed questions. Before running the experiment, think of a possible answer, or hypothesis. The experiment can test whether your hypothesis is correct.

A good question is one that you can answer by running a test and collecting data. Place your data in a graph so people can understand what you have discovered. As you do experiments, change only one thing, or variable, at a time. For example, you could test how quickly a robot navigates a maze using both touch sensors and infrared sensors. The type of sensor should be the only thing that is different between the two robots. Test each type several times and average the data (how long it took to get through the maze). Once you start running your robot, you can come up with many different experiments to try.

Get a notebook in which you can record information about each experiment you conduct. Date each entry so that you can keep track of when you did the experiment. List the materials you use, and keep notes on what you try and what results you observe. Add sketches or photos of designs and circuits that you use.

Safety First

1. Do any experiments or projects, whether from this book or of your own design, under the supervision of a science teacher or other knowledgeable adult.

2. Read all instructions carefully before proceeding with a project. If you have questions, check with an adult.

3. Maintain a serious attitude while conducting experiments. Fooling around can be dangerous to you and to others.

4. Wear approved safety goggles when you are doing anything that might cause injury to your eyes.

5. Do not put your fingers or any object other than properly designed electrical connectors into electrical outlets.

How to Use This Book

Chapters 2, 3, and 4 introduce you to the different components of robots. You will experiment with these parts and learn how they work. Then you will be ready to build you own robot, starting in Chapter 5.

What's Inside a Robot?

Robots have many different components (Figure 2.1). Some provide energy to operate other components; some transform that energy into motion; some use energy to sense the surrounding environment and to turn motors, lights, and sound on and off. The definition presented in the first chapter suggested what components are used to make robots. Let's look at these.

Some robots use hydraulic or pneumatic motors, but we will limit our robots to electric motors. There are many different kinds of electric motors (Figure 2.2), and you will learn which ones to use in different situations.

Mobile robots use batteries to supply power to their motors. Batteries supply direct current. Stationary robots, like those used in industry, can have alternating current motors, which get electricity from sockets. For example, your refrigerator at home gets its alternating current by plugging into a wall outlet. For this book, you will focus on direct current, or DC, motors.

If you have taken apart a motorized toy or if you have messed around with batteries and motors, you are

FIGURE 2.1

Robots use mechanical parts and electronic parts. Building and operating a robot will help you learn what many of these parts do.

FIGURE 2.2

Several different types of motors are used in robots. Servo motors, shown at the top, are most common. The other motors shown are (clockwise): DC motor, geared motor, and stepper motor.

FIGURE 2.3

Inside a servo motor are gears to reduce the speed of rotation and electronic circuits to control the motor.

familiar with inexpensive DC motors. Many run on voltages as low as 1.5 to 3, so a common battery or batteries can power them. These motors are inexpensive, but are not easy to use for robots. They rotate very fast: some spin as fast as 17,000 RPM (revolutions per minute). Think how fast you want the robot to travel (and still be able to control it). Any reasonable speed would require the wheels to turn much slower, maybe 100 RPM. To control the speed of the inexpensive motor, you either have to vary the current that powers the motor or you need to power the wheels through a set of reduction gears that slow the speed of rotation. In most robots, both approaches are used.

To reduce the current to a motor, it is better to rapidly turn it on and off rather than keeping it on at a lower level. Reducing the current puts stress on the motors, so it's better to turn the current fully on and off quickly to reduce the speed of the motor.

More commonly used in robots are servo motors (see Figure 2.3). Originally designed to operate the flaps and rudders in radio-controlled airplanes, servo motors have a DC motor and reducing gears inside a rectangular box. They also have electronic circuits that interpret the signals from a controlling computer to switch the motor on and off. You can identify servo motors by the number of connecting wires they have (three) and their rectangular shape. In most cases, servo motors will be best for your robots. Although they have low torque, or turning power, they can move very light robots.

Stepper motors are also used extensively in robots. You can recognize steppers by their more numerous wire connections (four to six) and their compact, cylindrical shape. Unlike common DC motors, steppers don't turn continuously when you power them. As their name implies, they take steps. One step turns the motor shaft a few degrees. They require a computer to provide signals to turn the motors one step at a time. The benefit of using steppers is the precision of their movements. They are used in printers and other machines that move a piece of paper or a print head a precise distance. If you find a stepper motor,

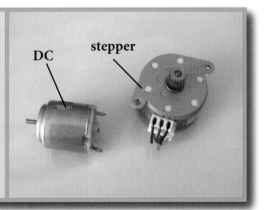

FIGURE 2.4

It's easy to tell a stepper motor from a DC motor. Steppers have a different shape and have four to six wires. DC motors have two leads for wires.

try rotating the driveshaft. Instead of smooth continuous motion, it will click-click-click as your turn the shaft—each click being one step.

Other types of motors are used in robots, too. Muscle Wire® shrinks when heated. Passing electrical current through the wire heats it, making it shrink in length. Turning off the current allows the wire to cool and elongate quickly, making the wire a simple motor for push-pull operations. Linear actuators also operate in a push/pull mode. If you have chimes for a doorbell, the device that hits the chimes is a linear actuator. An electromagnet inside pulls a metal rod through the chimes when the button is pushed. A spring pulls the rod back when the button is released.

Some robots don't use electric motors. Instead, they use hydraulic or pneumatic systems. If you have seen the giant, moving dinosaur models shown at museums, you have seen pneumatic, computer-controlled systems. In many exhibits, you can hear the air escaping from the pneumatic system.

In this book, you will use direct current motors and servo motors for driving your robot. They are inexpensive and easy to work with. Although this book suggests using servo motors as your drive motors, other motors that you find can be used for other functions on your robot. You can find these motors when you take old appliances apart.

Take Apart an Old Motorized Appliance

COOL!

You can find old appliances at thrift stores and garage sales. You might ask friends for any broken appliances that they are going to discard. Often, appliances fail due to bad switches, but the motors still work. Taking apart an appliance gives you an appreciation for how much engineering work goes into designing the appliance, and it helps you collect components (switches, motors, LEDs, and more) for your own projects.

1. Ask the owner of the appliance if you may have the appliance.

Things you will need

- **discarded VCR or other motorized appliance such as an electric typewriter**
- **screwdrivers—Phillips and flat**
- **wire cutters or scissors**
- **wire strippers**
- **9-volt battery**
- **pliers**
- **safety goggles**

2. Cut off the electric power cord with wire cutters and throw the cord away. This way, no one can inadvertently plug in the appliance while you are taking it apart.

3. Put on safety goggles to protect your eyes from springs and other small parts that may fly out while you are working.

4. Look for screws that hold the case together. Sometimes they are hidden under rubber feet or under stickers. Most common are Phillips screws, so your primary tool will be a Phillips screwdriver.

5. If you find a part that is not easy to remove, don't beat on it. Smashing the device won't help. If you use a flat screwdriver to pry it out, be careful to not aim that sharp edge at your hand, face, or other body part.

6. Be on the lookout for switches and motors. If you extract a motor, check any printing on the side for electrical power specifications. These will tell you if the motor uses DC voltage and can be powered by batteries and what voltage batteries you would need. Use wire strippers to remove the insulation from the ends of the motor's wire leads. Touch each lead to one of the two terminals on the top of a 9-volt battery to see if the motor works. It is quite likely that you will see the motor shaft spin and will hear the motor whir.

To power the motors and circuits on board, mobile robots carry batteries. For most applications, alkaline batteries work well. They provide constant voltage throughout the life of the battery and provide much longer life than traditional carbon zinc batteries. Rechargeable batteries are not good choices because their voltage drops as they are used. Onboard computers or microprocessors require a minimum voltage (usually 5 or 6 volts), and as rechargeable batteries lose charge, they provide lower voltages.

Most often robots require four batteries connected in series to deliver 6 volts. "Connected in series" means that each battery is connected to an adjacent battery, with the positive (+) side of one connected to the negative (−) side of the other. In series, the total voltage is the sum of the voltages of each battery connected. Four 1.5-volt batteries in series deliver 6 volts. On a robot, batteries are held in series in battery holders (Figure 2.5). These holders make it easier to attach the

Things you will need

- batteries (2 each of AA, AAA, C, and D cell)
- voltmeter or electronic multimeter
- masking tape or friend

batteries to the robot and to connect them to the robot. You will want to use a battery holder unless your microprocessor requires a battery with 9 volts or higher.

Gather a variety of batteries. You will need a voltmeter or electronic multimeter to measure their voltages. You can purchase these at electronic stores or online for a few dollars, or you may be able to borrow one from a science teacher at school.

1. Switch the meter to measure DC volts. If there are several ranges available, choose one that includes 0–12 volts.

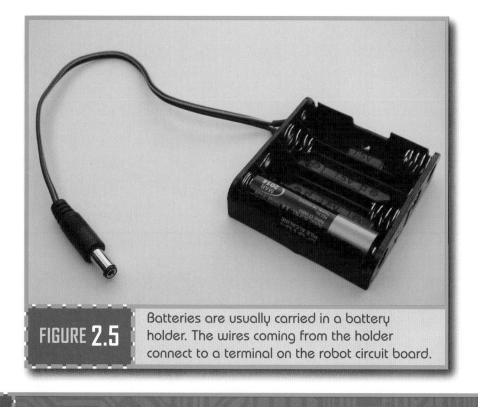

FIGURE 2.5　Batteries are usually carried in a battery holder. The wires coming from the holder connect to a terminal on the robot circuit board.

2. One of the meter leads will be red. Touch this one to the positive end of an AA, AAA, C, or D cell battery. If you're not sure which is the positive end, look at the side of the battery near each end for a + or – symbol. Touch the other lead, which is probably black, to the negative terminal of the battery. What does the meter show for the voltage?

3. All of the common cylindrical household batteries deliver 1.5 volts. If your battery is new, it might be able to deliver voltages above 1.5. If it has been used extensively, it will likely be showing a lower voltage. If the measured voltage is less than 1.3 volts, the battery is near the end of its life.

4. Try connecting two of the same type of battery together, in series, or head to tail. You could use a piece of masking tape to hold them together or get a friend to hold them while you make the measurement. What voltage do you measure with two batteries?

Idea for a Science Fair Project

Robot builders are always concerned with finding the best batteries. You could test different brands of batteries of the same voltage to see how long they last. Connect a fresh battery to a DC motor and let the motor spin. Stop the experiment either when the motor stops spinning or when the battery voltage drops to some value you determined in advance, say 75 percent of the battery's rated voltage.

Electronic Circuits

The heart of a robot is its onboard circuit board, which contains all the electronic components that control the robot's actions. You will need a circuit board for your robot (See the appendix for sources of circuit boards and robot systems.) The circuit board (Figure 2.6) is a piece of flat plastic with many electronic components mounted onto it. It needs electrical energy to run, so it must either have a battery on it or an electrical connection to a power source. With some boards, you can use an alternating current power supply—a detachable power cord that plugs into a wall outlet to provide power to electronic appliances. Many boards have an on-off switch between the source of power and the rest of the board.

Circuit boards have a central processing chip or microcontroller. This is the onboard computer. Most commonly you write programs on a personal computer (Figure 2.7) and download the code to the microcontroller. Downloading is accomplished either through a cable (serial cable or USB connection) or by infrared

FIGURE 2.6

The circuit board contains the robot's computer, memory, and other electronics.

FIGURE **2.7** — Programs for your robot are written on a personal computer and downloaded to the robot's microcomputer.

communication. If using infrared to download, an additional component is needed to send the signal. This "beamer" or sending unit connects to a personal computer either through a serial cable or USB port.

Programs aren't stored in the microcontroller, but in a separate memory chip mounted on the circuit board. EEPROM is a common memory chip technology. The letters stand for "*e*lectrically *e*rasable *p*rogrammable *r*ead-*o*nly memory." With no moving parts, this memory is quite reliable. It holds programs and data even when there is no power being supplied to the circuit board. When you turn the power back on, the microcontroller will get the most recent program from the EEPROM and start to execute it.

The circuit board controls motors, lights, and sound, and reads signals from sensors. A circuit board has input/output pins or ports that allow you to make connections to these devices. Some connectors consist of a series of slots you insert connecting wires to. Others are arrays of slots in the form of a breadboard, a plastic board with holes to which wires or pins (connected to sensors) connect or fit.

Circuit boards also have other components. Some are connectors, some are electronic components (resistors, capacitors, transistors), and others are integrated circuits. One type of robot circuit board, the Super Cricket board, comes with a piezoelectric speaker mounted on the board. This black cylinder with a small hole in the center is an electronic speaker that allows the board to make sounds and play songs. Both the Parallax, another type of circuit board, and the Super Cricket have reset buttons that allow you to restart the resident program. Look at the documentation that came with the board you have, or do an Internet search to see if you can find a guide that shows what each component is.

Sensors allow a robot to find its way along a path or to react to events around it. The simplest sensor is a touch switch (Figure 2.8). If a mobile robot runs into a wall and closes the switch, the robot can back up and change direction, then start again. Other sensors use light or infrared light to alert the robot that it is approaching a wall or obstacle.

1. Look at all the sensors around you as you move through a city, shopping mall, or school. Record them in your experiment notebook, writing down what the sensors do (or what you think they do) and how they operate.

2. At a road intersection, look for the sensors that trigger the traffic lights to change. There might be coils in the pavement; you can see the dark circles or rectangles where they were added after the pavement was laid. These coils act like giant metal detectors. Other sensors above the lights respond to infrared signals from emergency vehicles.

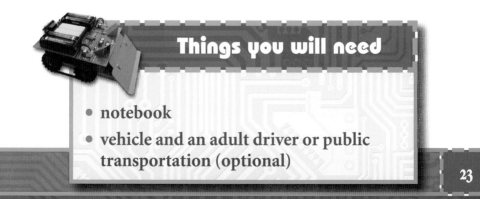

Things you will need

- notebook
- vehicle and an adult driver or public transportation (optional)

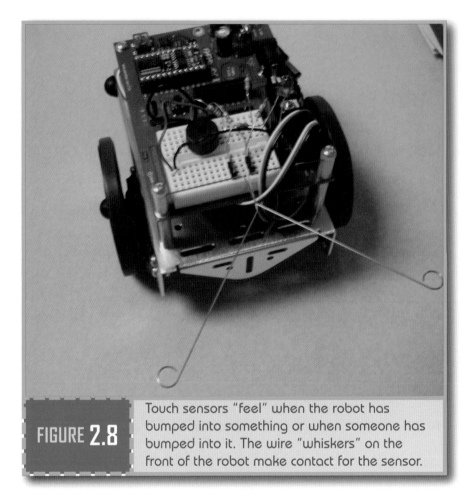

FIGURE **2.8** — Touch sensors "feel" when the robot has bumped into something or when someone has bumped into it. The wire "whiskers" on the front of the robot make contact for the sensor.

Some lights have cameras that record visible changes as cars pull up to the intersection.

3. Look for sensors in stores and other places, and record your observations. Any of these types of sensors could work with your robot. What would you have the sensors detect?

Control Servos with a Microcontroller

$\mathcal{E}$ach robot circuit board is designed to work with a specific set of software from a personal computer. (If you do not own a computer, ask to use one at school.) You can download this software either from a CD provided by your circuit board manufacturer or straight from the manufacturer's Web site. Downloading the software from the Internet is the better option. This software may contain improvements that are not on the CD that was shipped with the circuit board.

Once you have the software, follow the instructions to load it onto your computer. The computer you are using needs to know where to save the programs. If you are using a serial cable (a 9-pin connector) to connect to the robot (Figure 3.1), you may need to specify which com port to use. The com port is also called the serial port. If the software gives you the option, allow it to find the com port; otherwise, specify com port #1 under Preferences. Once you have the software installed, give it a try.

FIGURE 3.1

Use a cable (above) or infrared signals to download the program to your robot.

Connect a Servo Motor to the Circuit Board

1. For this first activity you will use a Parallax Board of Education (Boe-Bot®) with a Stamp 2 microcontroller. Connect a servo motor to the pin #12 servo connector marked on the board (Figure 3.2). Note that there are three other pin connectors for servo motors on the board. The beauty of these servo connectors is that no additional wiring is necessary: just push the end of the servo wires onto the three pins of connector #12. It *does* make a difference which way you plug the servo in. The black wire connected to the servo must connect to the pin that is marked "black" on the circuit board. Reversing this position will quickly ruin the servo motor—an event marked with the pungent smell of burning and possibly a small cloud of smoke. To avoid this, make sure you've plugged the servo in the right way. If you're not sure, get

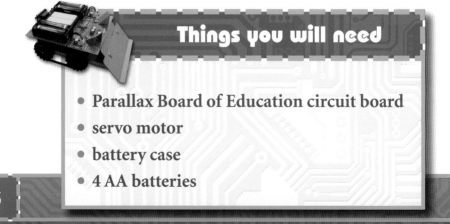

Things you will need

- **Parallax Board of Education circuit board**
- **servo motor**
- **battery case**
- **4 AA batteries**

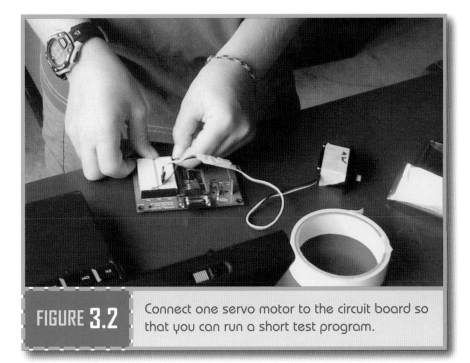

FIGURE 3.2 Connect one servo motor to the circuit board so that you can run a short test program.

someone else to confirm that you've got it right before you connect to power.

The red servo wire and pin connects to the positive (+) side of the battery case, and the black wire connects to the negative (−) side, or ground. The white wire in the middle connects to the microcontroller and carries the signals from the microcontroller to operate the servo.

2. Make the connection from the Boe-Bot board to your computer. Some boards come with serial cables and some come with USB connectors.

3. Use 4 AA batteries to power the circuit board. Some models have a "jumper" or connection you make depending on whether you are using battery power or an AC transformer/adapter. The jumper is located between the two sets of servo connectors on the board. Since you are using batteries, make sure that the jumper is connected to the pin closest to the printed Vin (which means "voltage in") or the voltage directly from the battery pack.

Insert the batteries into the battery pack, making sure you have them in the correct arrangement. Look at the inside of the pack for markings showing what direction each battery is supposed to go. If you're not sure, ask someone to check the arrangement before connecting the battery pack to the board. If one of the batteries is inserted backward, the output voltage won't be enough to power the robot and you will quickly ruin the batteries.

When you connect the battery pack to the board, note that the jack on the pack can fit into only one connector on the board. Insert it into the connector. If your board has a power switch, it will be located at the center bottom of the board. Slide the switch to the middle position and the LED (on the circuit board) should light. If it doesn't, recheck the batteries.

What happened? You might have noticed that the servo jumped when you connected the board to the battery pack. Did anything else happen?

The servo motor isn't turning! It's connected to power through the circuit board, but it is not spinning. For a servo motor to operate, it has to receive commands from the microprocessor on the circuit board. You will write a program that will make the motor run in section 3.3.

Continuous Rotation Servo Motors

Servo motors were originally developed to operate in a limited range of motion: they were intended to rotate less than 180 degrees. This works fine for controlling the flaps on a model airplane and steering a model car or boat, but doesn't work at all to drive a robot continuously in one direction. These "standard" servos can be changed to rotate continuously (keep moving in one direction), or you can purchase "continuous rotation servos." If you intend to make a mobile robot, it is best to purchase continuous rotation servos. If you have standard servos, do a Web search or look in the documents that came with your components for instructions for how to hack the servos. Get some experienced help to do this, as a mistake can destroy a servo.

Wheel Check

Wheels often present a big challenge for robot builders. There are thousands of wheels available, but what size and composition do you need, and how will they attach to the motors? Consider first how they attach.

Notice that servo motors have a plastic horn (Figure 3.3) attached to the driveshaft. This horn can have four or six arms or can be circular. It is held onto the servo motor two ways: a screw secures it, and it has ridges that match up with ridges on the servo motor driveshaft. These ridges, or splines, prevent the wheel from slipping on the driveshaft. The screw prevents the wheel from sliding off the shaft.

Attaching giant wheels to small servo motors will burn out the motors. Using tiny wheels might not carry the platform high enough off the ground. Wide wheels might be hard to turn, and smooth wheels might slide on slippery floors. Wheels that have rubber tires, usually O-rings, give good traction.

Things you will need

- Internet access
- notebook

FIGURE 3.3 Servo horns are small plastic or metal parts that fit onto the driveshaft of a servo motor. A screw goes through the center of the horn to attach it to the servo motor.

An ideal wheel would fit onto the servo motor driveshaft in place of the horn, and be secured in place with the same screw. These specialized wheels are sold with robot kits. Not as ideal, but adequate for most applications, is gluing a wheel to the servo horn. When looking at potential wheels, think about how you can get a good attachment to the horn.

1. Check out the wheels used by robots advertised on the Internet. Search for a robot store and look at the models

they sell. Look at the diameter and width of the wheels and whether they have tires mounted on them. See what you can learn from people who have solved the problem of wheels on robots. Take thorough notes on what you find.

2. Also look at substitutes for wheels. What other devices are robot manufacturers and builders using to support and propel their robots?

Idea for a Science Fair Project

Once your mobile robot is built and working, you could experiment with a variety of wheels to see which work best or provide the fastest travel. You could also experiment with using skids (cut from a piece of aluminum or other material) compared to casters. Does one allow for more consistent turns or faster travel?

Write a Program to Control a Servo

COOL!

1. To program a robot, you need the editing program from the manufacturer. You can get the Parallax Boe-Bot editor either from the Parallax Web site or from the CD that comes with the circuit board. Once the editor has been installed, open the Stamp editor.

2. In the editor window, type the following code:

```
'My first servo program
'This is to test the connection and servo
x var word
for x = 1 to 100
pulsout 12, 800
pause 20
next
end
```

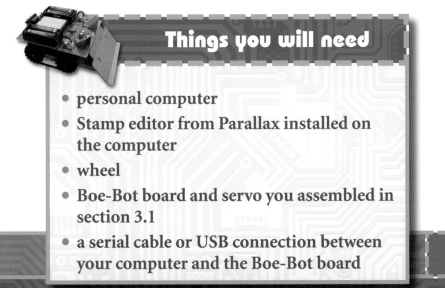

Things you will need

- personal computer
- Stamp editor from Parallax installed on the computer
- wheel
- Boe-Bot board and servo you assembled in section 3.1
- a serial cable or USB connection between your computer and the Boe-Bot board

3. When you have entered this code, run the program (push "run" from the Start menu or click on the black triangle in the tool bar). The immediate reaction will be a request from the computer to specify what type of microcontroller you are using. Most likely, it is a BS2, so click on that. (If you aren't sure, look at the microprocessor chip on the board. BS2, or some other model, will be printed on it.) The computer will add a line of code signifying that you are using the BS2 microcontroller.

4. If you typed the code in accurately, and if the connections are made correctly, the servo should turn for a few seconds. If that didn't occur and the computer didn't register any coding errors, the most likely problem is power. Make sure the batteries are good and that they are inserted correctly. If that doesn't solve the problem, recheck the servo connection. Is the servo plugged into the slot for pin 12? Is it inserted with the black wire toward the bottom of the circuit board?

   To rerun the program, you can either click on the black triangle again or push the reset button on the circuit board. Provided that the servo is a continuous rotation servo, it should rotate exactly as it did before.

Go back to the program and detail what each line of code did so that you can write your own programs (see Table 1). On the left is the code you entered, and on the right is an explanation of what the code means.

TABLE 1	My first program
Type this into computer	**Meaning of command**

`'My first program`
`'This is to test`
`the connection and`
`servo`
	Any line that starts with an apostrophe is a comment line that is ignored by the computer. Use comments to help you remember what you did.

`x var word`	Make *x* a variable and leave space in the memory for whatever numbers are assigned to *x*.
`for x = 1 to 100`	Set $x = 1$, process the following code up to the command "`next`".
`pulsout 12, 800`	Send a pulse of electricity to pin 12. The duration of that pulse is 800 ms times 2 or 1,600 ms. A ms is a millisecond, or 1/1,000 of a second.
`pause 20`	Pause 20 milliseconds.
`next`	This marks the end of the loop, go back to the "`for x = 1 to 100`" line, increase *x* by 1 and see if it is greater than 100. If it is greater, go to the first line of code following "`next`." Otherwise, execute the code between the "`for`" statement and the "`next`" statement again.
`end`	End of code

Here's what happens when you run this program. The "x var word" statement instructs the microcontroller to set aside space in the EEPROM memory on the circuit board for a variable, *x*. At this point, it doesn't know what values will be assigned to *x*, but it knows that it needs to reserve some space. In that line of code, "word" specifies how much space to set aside. The "word" command sets aside the most space possible; it can accommodate numbers up to 65,535, which is the limit for the Stamp chip.

The "for x = 1 to 100" starts a loop that will run 100 times. The microcontroller will keep count of how many times it completes the loop by increasing the value of *x* each time it comes back to this line. The "next" command is the end of the loop, so the program will execute the code between the "for..." and "next" statements 100 times.

There are only two lines of code that get repeated in this loop. The first sends a pulse of electricity to pin 12. If your servo is connected to pin 12, the servo will receive these pulses and will turn. Between each pulse, the voltage going to pin 12 is zero. During each pulse, the voltage is approximately 6 volts, or the voltage supplied by the batteries. Each pulse will last 1.6 milliseconds. Why 1.6? That was specified by the number 800. The computer interprets the "800" (in essence multiplying it by .002) as 1.6 milliseconds.

The "800" tells the microcontroller how far to turn and in what direction to turn. Using "900" instead of "800" will make it turn farther with each step. "950" will turn a bit farther, but not much farther. Don't use values greater than 950. Using values of 700 or less will rotate the servo motor in the opposite direction. Thus you can control both the direction and speed (somewhat) by your choice of values in the "pulsout" command. Don't use numbers smaller than 550 or larger than 950, as they might damage the servo motor.

After the microcontroller sends this pulse to the servo, it waits 20 milliseconds before going to the next line of code. You need to let a servo pause after receiving a pulse, so get in the habit of adding "pause 20" after each "pulsout" command.

Push the reset button again and notice which direction, clockwise or counterclockwise, the servo rotates. If you have trouble seeing the servo shaft rotate, put a wheel on the shaft.

Operate the Servo

1. Rewrite the program on your computer to make the servo motor rotate in the opposite direction. What will you have to change to get the servo to change directions? Make the change to the program, then download it and run it. Did it work?

2. Push the reset button again and notice low long the servo motor spins. How many seconds was it? If this were your finished robot and you wanted it to move twice as far, how would you change the program?

Things you will need

- personal computer
- Stamp editor from Parallax installed on the computer
- wheel
- Boe-Bot board and servo you assembled in section 3.1
- serial cable or USB connection between your computer and the Boe-Bot board

Double the Distance

COOL!

1. Rewrite the program on your computer to make the servo motor rotate for twice as long as it did initially. What do you need to change in your program? What controls how long the servo motor spins (how many pulses it receives)?

2. Trying different values in the "pulsout" command line gives you good information. Record the values you tried in your experiment notebook, along with how the servo motor responded.

Things you will need

- personal computer
- Stamp editor from Parallax installed on the computer
- wheel
- Boe-Bot board and servo you assembled in section 3.1
- serial cable or USB connection between your computer and the Boe-Bot board
- notebook and pencil

Find the Zero Value

If you've gotten your servo to spin in opposite directions by using different numbers in the "pulsout" command, there must be a number between the two you used where the servo doesn't spin at all. Can you find it?

1. Rewrite the program on your computer using the value in the "pulsout" command that will cause the servo not to spin. You could rewrite the program several times to get

Things you will need

- **personal computer**
- **Stamp editor from Parallax installed on the computer**
- **wheel**
- **Boe-Bot board and servo you assembled in section 3.1**
- **serial cable or USB connection between your computer and the Boe-Bot board**
- **masking tape**
- **marker**
- **small Phillips screwdriver**

closer and closer to the zero movement value, but can you rewrite the program once so that it finds the zero value or center point? To do this, you can use the value for *x* in the "for" statement as the value in the "pulsout" statement. For example,

```
for x = 650 to 850 step 10
pulsout 12, x
pause 100
next
```

This will drive the servo starting at 650 and increase the value of *x* by 10 each time through the program. The longer pause gives you time to count along with the program so you know where the zero value is. Remember, however, to operate the servo motors only in the range of 550 to 950.

2. What value for the "pulsout" command doesn't turn the servo motor? Record this value in a notebook you keep for your robot experiments. Since the values you find for different servo motors are likely to be different, mark the servo motor to identify it from other servo motors (using masking tape and a marker).

3. Many servos are centered on or near the value 750. At values higher than 750, the servos rotate in one direction, and below 750, they rotate in the other direction. If your

FIGURE 3.4 You can change the center or no-move point of a servo motor by turning the small Phillips screw in the servo motor.

servo motor is not "centered" at 750, you may be able to adjust it with a small Phillips screwdriver. Look on your servo for a small hole in the case with a screw inside. If it has this hole and screw inside, you can adjust the center point for your servo (see Figure 3.4).

4. Rerun the first program using 750 in the "`pulsout`" command. While the servo is turning, use a small Phillips screwdriver to rotate the screw inside the servo. Turn the screw so that the servo doesn't turn when the program is running.

Idea for a Science Fair Project

You know that each servo has a center value where it won't spin, and that the farther the value is away from that center, the faster the servo will spin. Measure how fast a servo spins for a range of values. Mark the servo horn with a piece of masking tape. For each test, count the number of times the horn completes a circle in 15 seconds. Multiply this number by 4 to get the revolutions per minute. Start at the center value, the point where the servo won't spin. This speed is zero. Then increase the value by 5 units and repeat the test. Record the results for later graphing. Keep increasing the value by 5 units until the output speed isn't changing. Start over, this time decreasing the value by 5 units. When you graph the results (speed of rotation vs. the "`pulsout`" value), show clockwise rotations as positive values and counterclockwise as negative. Put into words what the graph tells you.

Test Another Servo Motor

After marking the first servo motor with a name or number, disconnect it and connect a second servo motor to the same pin slot (Figure 3.5). Test it to see if it runs and where its center value is. Mark this servo and record its center value in your experiment notebook, or, if it has an adjustment screw, center it at the value of 750.

Things you will need

- personal computer
- Stamp editor from Parallax installed on the computer
- wheel
- Boe-Bot board and servo you assembled in section 3.1
- serial cable or USB connection between your computer and the Boe-Bot board
- masking tape
- marker, notebook, and pencil
- small Phillips screwdriver
- second servo motor

FIGURE 3.5 Once you have tested one servo motor and gotten it to work, test the other servo motor.

Operate Standard Servos

The Super Cricket is another type of robot system (Figure 3.6). The Super Cricket circuit board has eight servo motor ports, which means you can use it to control eight servos. The programming code is written for standard servos rather than continuous rotation servos. That is, the program specifies both the servo identification (or port number) and the desired final position. Servo ports are numbered 1 to 8, and servo positions are numbered 0 to 255. Position 0 has the servo rotated fully counterclockwise, and position 255 has it rotated fully clockwise. The statement for operating servos is:

```
servo <port number> <position value>
```

Things you will need

- computer
- Super Cricket board and infrared beamer
- standard servo motor (at least one)
- wheel or servo horn
- masking tape
- marker
- notebook and pencil

FIGURE **3.6**

The Super Cricket circuit board comes with an infrared beamer. The beamer connects to the computer on which you wrote the robot program. It uses infrared signals to download the program to the Cricket.

To operate a standard servo motor in port 3 with a value of 127, the statement would be:

    servo 3 127

1. Plug a standard (not continuous rotation) servo into port 3. Make sure you follow the labels when wiring the servo. Find the letters "blk" on the Super Cricket and ensure that the black servo wire connects to the pin in that column.

2. Download the software for the Cricket Logo Program from

the Handyboard Web site. Then copy the following code into the Cricket Logo Program window of the software:

```
to runservos
beep
wait 5
servo 3 127
end
```

3. Click on the Download button with the Cricket facing the infrared beamer. You should see the LEDs on both boards flash. When the downloading is finished, type the program name, "runservos," into the Command Center window and hit return. The Cricket should beep, wait half a second, and then the servo should rotate and stop.

   If you connected a continuous rotation instead of a standard servo to port 3, the servo would keep turning. The sensor inside the servo will never sense that the servo has reached position 127, so it will keep turning. To get it to stop, turn the power switch off on the Cricket.

   The first line in the program identifies it from any other programs you may write. The second line makes the piezoelectric speaker make a sound (beep). The third line has the Cricket wait 5 time units, each unit being 0.1 seconds. The fourth line directs the servo connected to pin 3 to turn to position 127.

4. Play around with the program to control a standard servo, changing the values for the position. Replace the 127 in the program with another number from 0 to 255. Watch which way the servo rotates. If you're having trouble seeing the servo shaft rotate, mount a wheel or servo horn onto the shaft.

5. Record in your experiment notebook what happens. If you have different types of servos, try each and record your results. Make sure you mark the servo motors so that you can identify each one and relate it to the results in your notebook.

3.9

Operate Continuous Rotation Servos

Continuous rotation servos will run well on the Super Cricket. The only difference between running them and running standard servos is that the program has to turn the continuous rotation servos off. The command to turn off a servo plugged into port 3 is:

```
offservo 3
```

1. Type the following program into the Cricket Logo Programs window, download it, and run it. Connect a continuous rotation servo motor to pin 6. Make sure that the program name is in the Command Center window. Note that we used the same name for this program as the one in section 3.8. When you download this one, it will overwrite the previous code in the memory.

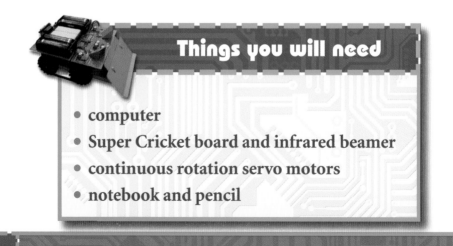

Things you will need

- **computer**
- **Super Cricket board and infrared beamer**
- **continuous rotation servo motors**
- **notebook and pencil**

```
to runservos
beep
wait 5
servo 6 200
wait 5
offservo 6
end
```

2. Try different values for the "wait" command and in the "servo 6" line. Record your results in your experiment notebook. What direction does the servo spin at large servo position numbers (such as 200)? What direction does it spin at small position numbers (such as 35)? Find the position number where the servo doesn't turn at all. Record this number along with a name for the servo.

3. Repeat this experiment with other continuous rotation servos. Mark the servos so that you can identify them and relate the servo to the data you have recorded in your notebook.

1. The Super Cricket can also run DC motors. On the board you can see locations for motors marked A, B, C, and D. If you have a DC motor that has a plug attached to the leads, insert it into one of the four motor ports. (You can order DC motors with plugs from Gleason Research, or you can get the plugs and wires from Gleason and wire your own motors.)

2. With the motor wired into motor port A, type the following code into the Cricket Logo Program window:

```
to runmotors
beep
wait 5
A, onfor 10
end
```

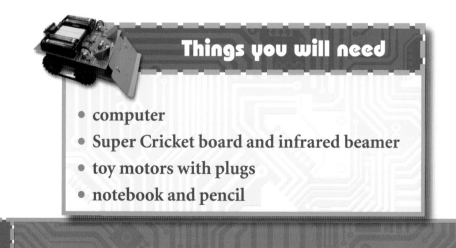

Things you will need

- **computer**
- **Super Cricket board and infrared beamer**
- **toy motors with plugs**
- **notebook and pencil**

3. Download this program and run it, having typed the program name into the Command Center window. You can command one to four motors with the same commands. List the lettered port followed by a comma and a space. To turn on motors A and C for one second, you use the code:

```
AC, onfor 10
```

If you want the motor(s) on indefinitely, use "on" instead of "onfor 10." The command "rd" reverses the direction of the motor(s). Bring the motors to a stop before reversing their direction by using the "offservo <servo port number>" command.

4. Start with the program you just entered and change the numerical values. Record your results in your experiment notebook.

Once your robot is mobile, you can try sumo wrestling with robots. Two robots start in a circular area (the ring) with the objective of pushing the other robot out of the circle. Adding sensors to detect the other robot and the edge of the ring makes it more fun. (Figure 3.7)

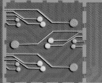

FIGURE 3.7 Mobile robots can compete with others in sumo contests.

Robot Sounds

What does a robot sound like? Any way you want it to! Microcontrollers can generate a variety of electronic signals at a wide range of frequencies. Converted into sound by a speaker, these signals can be audible.

Of course, it's a long way from making a noise at a single frequency to making voices or playing a song, but you can weave noises into interesting patterns and even into simple melodies.

Human hearing occurs in a very limited range, from a few tens of cycles per second (called Hertz) through 15,000 to 18,000 Hertz. A note played at 25,000 Hertz may get the attention of dogs, but not humans. Most conversations occur in the range of a few hundred Hertz to a few thousand Hertz. This is where humans hear best, so this is the range to use in making sounds you want people to hear.

Piezoelectric Speakers

Watches, cell phones, microwave ovens, and other appliances that make tones at only one or a few frequencies use piezo-electric speakers (Figure 4.1). These speakers are made from a type of crystal that vibrates when an electrical voltage is

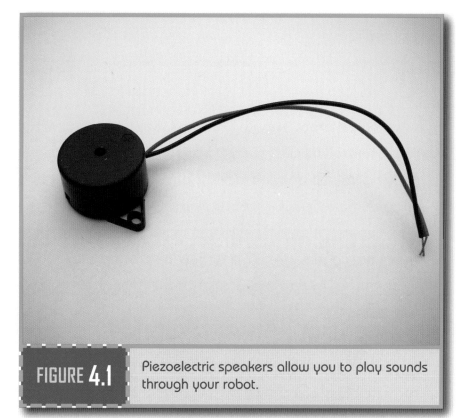

FIGURE 4.1 Piezoelectric speakers allow you to play sounds through your robot.

applied to it. (They also work in reverse, creating an electric spark when the crystal is compressed. Gas stoves have piezoelectric starters to ignite the burner when the gas is turned on.) They are inexpensive and easy to use, but they don't generate loud sounds, and the sound quality isn't great.

Many robot kits include piezoelectric speakers. The Super Cricket has one mounted on the circuit board. With the Parallax Boe-Bot kit, the speaker comes as a component to be inserted onto the breadboard (the white rectangle with rows of holes).

Piezoelectric speakers must be connected in the correct direction. Usually you can find a + near the leg that is to be connected to the positive pin. The other leg is connected to the negative side of the battery case, Vss, which is referred to as "ground."

Programming sounds is easy. One command is all that is required. For the Parallax system, the command is "`freqout`," for "frequency output." The command looks like this:

```
freqout 3, 500, 3000
```

This command directs the microcontroller to send an electronic signal to pin 3. The signal is to stay on for 500 milliseconds (0.5 second, or half a second). The frequency of the signal is 3,000 Hertz (or cycles per second).

Make Sounds

1. Connect the positive (+) leg of the speaker to an unused pin in the row of black pins of the circuit board. Connect the other speaker leg to any empty row of the breadboard. (The breadboard is the large white rectangle on the circuit board.) Use a piece of wire from the kit to connect another pin in the same row of the breadboard to one of the slots marked Vss. Vss completes the circuit by connecting it to the negative side of the battery case. The positive side of the battery case supplies power through the pin.

2. Write a simple program to play a note. Use the "freqout" command described above. Try changing values for both the frequency of the sound and its duration. What is the highest sound frequency you can hear? What is the lowest? Record these values in your notebook.

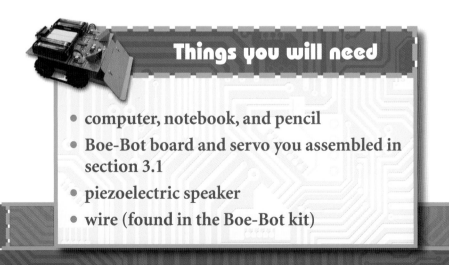

Things you will need

- computer, notebook, and pencil
- Boe-Bot board and servo you assembled in section 3.1
- piezoelectric speaker
- wire (found in the Boe-Bot kit)

Cascading Sounds

1. With a piezoelectric speaker connected to your robot, write the following code and download it to the robot:

(Program to enter)	(Notes for you)
`'Program to make cascading sounds`	Use the apostrophe to make a comment that identifies the program.
`x var word`	Tells the microcontroller to leave storage space in memory of a variable called x. The "`word`" command specifies how much room to leave.
`for x = 500 to 5000 step 500`	Launches a loop that sets $x = 500$ and has x increase by increments of 500 (step 500) until x reaches 5,000.
`freqout 3, 500, x`	Each time through the loop, the robot will send an electronic signal to pin 3 (where the speaker is connected). The signal will last for 500 milliseconds and will be at frequency x.
`next`	At the end of the loop: go back to the "`for x =`" statement and step up x by 500.
`end`	End

Things you will need

- computer
- Boe-Bot board and servo you assembled in section 3.1, and wire
- piezoelectric speaker
- serial cable or USB connection

2. Now try some variations of this program. You can vary the size of the step or change the frequency range below 500 or above 5,000. Try changing the duration (500 milliseconds in this example). Then try introducing a second variable, y. Make it equal to some mathematical formula based on x. For example, y could equal 10x. Try some creative variations.

If you can find or know the musical notes for a simple song, you can program them into your robot. Your robot could play "Happy Birthday"! Here are a few notes and their frequency equivalents (in Hertz).

Note	C	D	E	F	G	A	B	C
Frequency (Hz)	262	294	330	349	392	440	494	523

One use of a piezoelectric speaker is to help you identify what part of the program the robot is executing. You might have it emit one blast when the program launches (to alert you to a potentially low battery) and two blasts later in the program. Knowing what the program is doing helps you figure out if it is working properly.

The Super Cricket has the piezoelectric speaker mounted on its circuit board. To get it to make a sound, type the command "beep" in the Command Center on the Cricket Logo programming window and hit return.

Try writing a program in the Cricket Program Logo window. Copy this code into the window:

```
to beep1
repeat 5 [beep wait 4]
end
```

Click on the Download button, making sure that the Cricket and its infrared beamer are facing each other.

When the program has loaded onto the Cricket, type "beep1" (the name of the program) in the Command Center and hit return. You should hear 5 beeps, each separated by 0.4 seconds.

Here is another way to get the Cricket to make repeated noise. Type the following in the program window:

```
to beep2
loop [beep wait 5]
end
```

This program sends a never-ending string of beeps, each separated by a half-second pause.

Idea for a Science Fair Project

Find a simple song and program your robot to play it. For others to hear, you will need to amplify the sounds. Replace the piezo speaker with an amplifier/speaker available at electronics stores.

1. Like the Parallax system, the Super Cricket allows you to play specific tones. Use the "`note`" command. After typing the command, leave one space, and then type the pitch number, another space, and then the duration (in tenths of seconds). In the program screen type it will look like this:

   ```
   to tone1
   note 150 8
   wait 9
   note 300 5
   end
   ```

2. After downloading this program, type the program name, `tone1`, in the Command Center and hit return. You should hear two different tones, separated by nearly one second.

3. Make a program that plays a simple tune. Use the "`note`" and "`beep`" commands. Here is a table of pitch numbers

Things you will need

- **computer**
- **Super Cricket board and beamer**
- **wire**

(Different from the frequency of the note, pitch numbers are a code used in Crickets.) and their musical equivalent for the octave between middle C and high C:

Pitch number	119	105	94	89	79	70	62	59
Note	C1	D	E	F	G	A	B	C2

The Super Cricket allows you to download a program with variables and later specify the value of those variables. In the example that follows, *n* is a variable that isn't specified until you run the program. Each time you run the program, you can change the value of *n*.

4. Type the following program into the program screen:

```
to beepy :n
repeat :n [beep wait 5]
end
```

This tells Cricket to expect a value for the variable *n*, which will be the number of times it must repeat the commands. The commands are to beep and wait half a second. Download this program. In the Command Center, type:

```
beepy :6
```

and press return. Cricket should beep 6 times with a half-second pause between each. By specifying "6" in the run command, you have the program replace the *n* with a 6.

Build Your Robot

t's time to build your robot. What do you want it to do? If you want it to move across the floor, it should be fairly small and light (Figure 5.1). It will probably have two drive wheels, each powered by a servo motor, and a following wheel or skid. Alternatively, it could walk or use tanklike treads called tracks (Figure 5.2), but the easiest way is to use a two-wheel drive system.

If you want your robot to be stationary and operate motors, lights, and sounds, you will need a solid base or platform on which to attach the hardware. Mobile robots, however, often take more planing and care to design.

Platforms

In cars, the metal frame provides the structure to which all the components attach. In a robot, the frame is called a platform. Its purpose is to hold everything your robot will need to perform (Figure 5.3). If your robot will be a

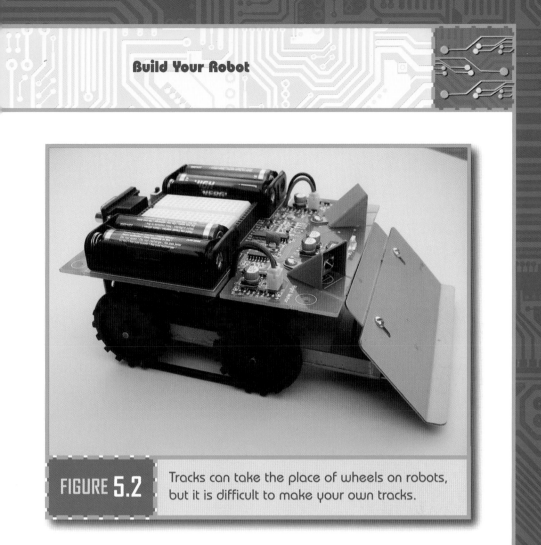

FIGURE 5.2 Tracks can take the place of wheels on robots, but it is difficult to make your own tracks.

nimble mobile bot, the platform should be small and easy to maneuver. If its job is to move materials or throw things, it should be bigger and sturdier to hold the additional motors. Platforms are the least expensive parts of your robot, and you might need to make several to allow your robot to perform different tasks.

What material should you use to make a platform? The best answer is any material you can get, cut, and shape. Platforms need to provide a solid and stiff base for the motors

FIGURE **5.3** The platform needs to be made of light, easy-to-work material that provides enough strength to hold the components securely.

to attach to. Since you will be attaching things to them, the material should be easy to screw into or through. Many platforms are made of aluminum; some are made of plastic; and some are even made of thin plywood. Plastic can carry static electricity that can damage sensitive electronic components—but such damage is uncommon. Sheets of PVC plastic that are ¼ inch thick are a good material for platforms. They are easy to cut and shape and easy to use for screw-mounting.

Plywood works as well, and ¼-inch thickness will be strong enough for most mobile robots. For very small robots, you could go with thinner wood, but you will not be able to screw components onto it as the screws would not hold. Thicknesses much larger than ¼ inch will be very heavy for the small servo motors to push around. Aluminum or other sheet metal also works if you have the tools to cut and shape it.

You might have old toys or parts of appliances that you could use for platforms. Look around to see what materials you have available.

How big should the platform be? Making it large will put more stress on the motors and may make it difficult to navigate in tight spaces. Making it too small will make it difficult to fit on the components you want. Begin with a rectangle about 6 inches long and 4 inches wide.

Robots with two-wheel drive steer differentially. Unlike a car that has a steering wheel that controls the position of the front wheels, differential steering works by having each wheel turn at a different speed. To go forward, both wheels have to turn in the same direction at the same speed. (But since the two servo motors are on opposite sides of the platform and are facing opposite directions, one will have to turn clockwise and the other counterclockwise to move forward.) To turn left, the wheel on the right has to rotate faster than the wheel on the left. Think of the two wheels and how many different ways you could control them to make a left turn.

Without gyroscopes or other stabilizing mechanisms, your robot will need either a third wheel or a skid. A small caster (a wheel that can rotate around its base as well as roll forward and backward) works well (Figure 5.4). A less expensive option is to mount a regular small wheel (but not a caster). Unless you can convert it into a caster, it will drag across the floor when the robot is turning. Usually this is not a problem, but on some floor surfaces it could be. Even simpler is a skid—a strip of sheet metal bent into the shape of the letter C. This will support the end of the robot and drag across the floor. Any of these will work, but the caster is probably the best option.

FIGURE 5.4

A caster or wheel that can swivel makes a good third support for a mobile robot.

Lay Out Your Robot

1. Place the circuit board for your robot on a piece of graph paper (Figure 5.5). Trace around the outside of the board, making the outline bigger than the board on all sides. This outline will act as a stencil for your platform that you will build.

2. Move the board off the paper. Hold the servo motors over the paper where you think you will want them on the platform. They should be directly opposite each other,

Things you will need

- microprocessor circuit board
- graph paper
- notebook and pencil
- servo motors with wheels
- tape measure or ruler
- wood, plastic, or sheet metal for platform
- saw or snips for cutting out platform
- sandpaper or metal file

- square
- drill
- pliers
- screws
- screwdriver
- glue
- third wheel or skid
- hammer and nail
- battery holder
- tape
- strip of thin metal

FIGURE 5.5 Use a piece of graph paper to decide what size the platform should be.

positioned so that they support much of the weight of the robot. Make pencil marks showing the outline of the servos in the position you want. Note that since each one attaches to a wheel on the outside of the platform, they will be facing in opposite directions.

3. Hold the wheels next to the servos to see how they will fit. Do you need to cut indents to accommodate the wheels? Do you know how you will attach the wheels to the servos?

If the wheels came with the servos, you can use the screw that holds the plastic horn on the servo shaft to hold them in place. You will be able to slide the wheel onto the shaft and screw it in place. However, if the wheel doesn't fit onto the servo shaft, you might have to attach each wheel to one of the servo horns that fit onto the shaft of a servo motor. The horns come with the servo motors and are held in place with a screw. You can glue the wheel to a horn and then reattach and screw the horn to the shaft. Think about this detail now to see if it will impact how you position the servos.

4. How will you attach the servos to the platform? Gluing them isn't the best solution. It's better to screw them into a piece of wood or other material that is itself glued and screwed to the platform. This allows you to replace a servo if it fails.

5. Where will the battery case go? You could mount it underneath the platform, provided that it won't drag on the ground. This positioning saves space. Will the battery wires reach the circuit board where they need to plug in? Will you need to drill a hole through the platform to accommodate the battery wires? Where should the hole be and how large should it be?

6. Try to imagine how much weight you want on the servo wheels as opposed to on the third wheel or skid. Most of the weight should go on the servo wheels so that they have good traction. Decide where you want the third wheel or skid to go, and mark that on the paper. You can change the drawing of your platform as needed; that's the beauty of doing it on paper first.

7. Do you have ideas for other components that will need to go on the platform? If you want the robot to navigate autonomously, it will need touch sensors or infrared sensors. How will you mount them? Usually you need two sensors, one on each side of the forward-moving robot. They need to be positioned so that they see or encounter different objects. If the robot is coming to a wall on the left side, you want only the left sensor to be activated. If the wall is directly in front of the robot, both sensors need to be activated at the same time. Hold the sensors you will use on the paper design of your robot. Decide where you want them positioned and how you will attach them to the platform.

8. If your robot will carry a gripper (Figure 5.6) or other motorized assemblies, sketch these onto the design of the bot. Think about the weight of these additional assemblies

FIGURE 5.6 Grippers give a robot the ability to pick up light objects. You can make your own or purchase some ready to be installed.

and the balance of the bot. Having a large weight hanging over the front or side of the robot may cause it to tip over. How will you attach these assemblies?

Lots of questions! You may not have all the answers yet. That's okay. Sketch on the paper what you think will work. As you build and operate the robot, your design will change. That's the beauty of robots! They are designed to

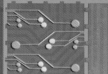

do different things, so tomorrow's design might be quite different from today's.

Tape your sketch to the wall so that you see it often and will think about it. Write down design information on the sketch. Once the robot is built, save the sketch by taping it into your experiment notebook. It's always fun to see how different the final design is from the initial design.

9. With your design in hand, get the measurements from the paper and lay them out on the material you are going to cut for the platform. Get someone who is experienced to help you cut out the platform with a saw or snips. After cutting, sand or file the edges to remove sharp or rough edges. Now you're ready to position the servo motors.

10. Take the time to get the servo motors positioned as precisely as possible. You want the robot to have wheels that are parallel to each other. This isn't easy to do. Use a square to help draw lines on the platform to guide you in placing the servos. It is common to screw the servos into a small piece of wood that is screwed or glued to the platform. If you're going to do this, cut the wood, mark on the wood where the screws will go, and get help making starter holes (with a small bit in a drill). Screw the

FIGURE 5.7 Attach the circuit board to the top surface of the platform.

servos into the wood blocks and align the blocks on the platform. When you are sure that the servos are in line and that the wheels will be parallel to each other, secure the blocks to the platform.

11. Add the third wheel or skid. If using a skid, use a hammer and nail to punch a hole through a strip of thin metal that is 7 to 10 cm (3 to 4 in) long and 1 cm (½ in) wide. Screw through this hole into the underside of the platform. Bend the strip so that it will drag along the floor, keeping the platform level (the same height as the servo wheels are holding it). You want the open end of the C facing the rear so the end of the skid won't hit the ground.

12. Screw the battery holder to the platform. Drill any holes you need to get the battery cable to the circuit board. Secure the circuit board to the platform (Figure 5.7), following your design. It's a good idea to have the circuit board raised above the platform to provide cooling air-flow and to make sure that the platform doesn't short out any of the contacts on the bottom of the circuit board.

13. Now attach the wheels to the servos. Connect the servo wires to the circuit board. Tape the servo wires down so that they don't get caught on anything. You're ready to test your robot.

1. Insert batteries in the battery case, making sure they are in the correct position. Connect the battery cable to the circuit board. Make sure that you have power by checking any LEDs on board. Now write a program to move the robot forward.

2. Use the same code you used to test the servos in section 3.3. The only change is that you need one additional line of code for the second servo. The new line of code will be almost the same as the "`pulsout`" code for the first servo. The difference will be that you need to specify whatever pin the second servo is connected to. In our example, the first servo was connected to pin #12, so the second one could be connected to pin # 13, 14, or

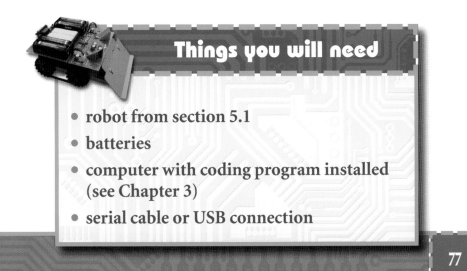

Things you will need

- robot from section 5.1
- batteries
- computer with coding program installed (see Chapter 3)
- serial cable or USB connection

15. Another difference will be that the second servo has to spin in the opposite direction. Why? Look at the two servos. One is facing to the right and the other is facing to the left. If both spin in a clockwise direction, they will turn the robot. To make the robot go forward, one has to spin clockwise and the other counterclockwise. So one will have a "`pulsout`" argument above the center point (nominally 750) and the other will be below it. They should be about equal values away from the center point: if one is 150 above 750 (making it 900), the other should be 150 below 750 (600). Remember to keep your range between 550 and 950. Also remember to use a pause 20 after the two "`pulsout`" commands—one pause statement will be enough for both "`pulsout`" commands. The "`pause`" command allows the servo motors time to reset after operating.

3. Write the code. Download it to the robot and watch what happens. Disconnect the download cable so that the robot can run freely. Did the robot go in a straight line? Did it go forward? What do you need to change to make it to work the way you want it to?

4. Try some different numbers in the "`pulsout`" command to see how the robot behaves.

Control the Motion

Now make the robot travel in a straight line, exactly one meter.

1. Put some tape on the floor to mark the start and stopping lines for a 1-meter track.

2. Place your robot on the start line and hit the Reset button. The Reset button restarts the program from the first line. Did it reach the stop line?

3. If the robot turns to one side, first check that the wheels are parallel and that the servo motors are securely attached. If they are, adjust the "`pulsout`" arguments to speed up one servo or slow down the other one. Making

Things you will need

- **mobile robot from section 5.2**
- **computer**
- **masking tape**
- **measuring tape**
- **notebook and pencil**
- **serial cable or USB connection**

the numbers closer to the center point (750) will slow them down. The servo motors don't respond linearly to these changes. They exhibit large changes in speed very close to the center point and very small changes the farther away from the center the number becomes. Going from 900 to 925 might result in no noticeable change in speed, while going from 760 to 785 will cause a big change in speed.

4. Record in your experiment book the values for each servo when the robot drove in a straight line. Also record how many loops (for x = 1 to ?) it took to go exactly 1 meter. These numbers will be helpful to you later, so be sure to record them beside the appropriate servo name or number.

Idea for a Science Fair Project

As you watch your robot move across the floor, do the wheels slip? If the tires or wheels lose grip, the robot might not go as far each time you run it, or it might turn instead of going straight. You could test a variety of tires or wheels to see which provides the best traction on one type of floor, or you could test a variety of floor surfaces.

Make a Left Turn

COOL!

Going only in a straight line isn't helpful. Your robot will need to turn. How do you make it turn?

1. Save the program you wrote for section 5.3. Then write a new program that will turn the robot 90 degrees to the left. How will you do this?

2. If you're not sure, pretend your shoes are the wheels on the robot. If you want to go forward, shuffle both feet forward. But to turn, what do you do? You could shuffle the right foot forward and not move (only rotate) the left foot. Or you could shuffle the left foot backward and not move (only rotate) the right foot. Or you could shuffle both feet forward, but shuffle the right foot much faster. Can you figure out other ways to turn left?

Things you will need

- **mobile robot from section 5.3**
- **computer**
- **masking tape**
- **measuring tape**
- **notebook and pencil**
- **serial cable or USB connection**

3. Decide how you want the robot to execute a turn, and then write the code. Remember that "`pulsout`" numbers above the center point (750) turn a servo in one direction and numbers below that point turn it in the opposite direction.

4. Keep experimenting with the code to find the "`pulsout`" values that give the turn you like best. Then record those values in your experiment book. Every time you want your robot to turn left, you can look up to see what values for the "`pulsout`" and the "`for x = 1 to · · ·`" commands you need.

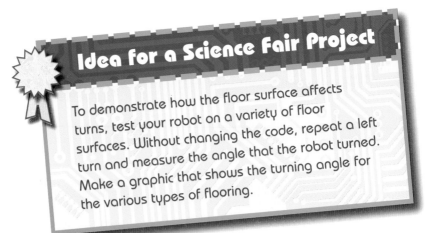

Idea for a Science Fair Project

To demonstrate how the floor surface affects turns, test your robot on a variety of floor surfaces. Without changing the code, repeat a left turn and measure the angle that the robot turned. Make a graphic that shows the turning angle for the various types of flooring.

Run the Square

COOL!

How can you make the robot travel in a square that has 1-meter-long sides (Figure 5.8)? You want the robot to end up exactly where it started.

1. Write a program that will drive the robot in a complete square. The microcontroller will execute each line of the program, line by line, so keep adding commands in the order you want them executed. Have the robot move forward, turn left, move forward, turn left, and continue so that it ends up where it started. You have already written code for both of these tasks, so this experiment challenges you to put the two sets of code together.

Things you will need

- mobile robot from section 5.4
- computer
- masking tape
- measuring tape
- notebook and pencil
- serial cable or USB connection

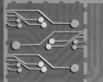

FIGURE 5.8 Lay out a 1-meter square on the floor. Program your robot to travel around the square and back to the start.

2. When the robot has completed the square, count the number of lines of code it took. Elegance in programming is doing the most with the fewest lines of code. Can you think of a way to greatly reduce the number of lines of code?

When you wanted the robot to move forward, it required many individual "`pulsout`" commands. If you had to write each command as a separate line, the program would have been hundreds of lines long. Instead, you used a loop. The microcontroller executed the loop as many times as you specified in the "`for x = 1 to . . .`" command. Since you want the robot to do the same thing four times (go forward and turn left to complete the square), add a second loop. To do this you will need another variable. Having two "`for x = 1 to . . .`" commands will confuse the microcontroller. Add a second variable, y, as the loop variable, and have y go from 1 to 4. Remember that the program needs to specify variables at the start. Look at your programs; there is a line that looks like this:

```
x var word
```

You need a similar statement for the variable y. And, like the x variable declaration, this needs to be at the top of the program.

3. Rewrite the code using two loops. See whether it works by running the new program in your robot. Then count the number of lines of code that this program needed. Saving lines of code gives you the opportunity to do more within the limited memory of the robot.

4. Record this program in your notebook.

Idea for a Science Fair Project

Building a robot is a great start for a science fair project. Now find a way you can experiment with it. You should test how changes in the programs you write make the robot respond faster or slower. Or you could test different switches, LEDs, or servo motors. Ideally, you will come up with an experiment that gives you numerical values that you can display in graphs or compare as statistical measures (averages, for example).

Control LEDs

Robots most often use LEDs, or light-emitting diodes, instead of incandescent lights (Figure 6.1). LEDs draw much less current than other lightbulbs, so they don't drain the batteries as quickly. And they last for a long time.

Diodes are electronic components that pass electricity in one direction but not the other. Thus to work, an LED must be connected correctly.

FIGURE 6.1 LEDs, light-emitting diodes, are easy to use with your robot.

Look at some LEDs. (If you don't have any, you can see them or purchase them online or at electronic stores.) You will see that one of the two wire legs is longer than the other. The convention with diodes is that the longer leg connects to the positive (+) side. On microcontrollers, the positive side of the batteries is connected through the pins, so the longer leg will connect to a pin.

LEDs have very high resistance until the current flows. Then the resistance drops dramatically. With little resistance in a circuit, the current can be quite high, even in a low-voltage circuit. Ohm's law specifies the relationship between voltage, current, and resistance:

$$I = V/R, \quad \text{or} \quad \text{current} = \text{voltage} / \text{resistance}$$

This law states that the current (I) is equal to the voltage in the circuit divided by the resistance (R). Take a simple example. Assume that a circuit has a resistance of 1 ohm and is powered by a battery pack with 4 fresh AA batteries. The voltage will be 6 volts, and the equation becomes:

$$I = 6 \text{ volts}/1 \text{ ohm}$$

Solving for the current, I, gives 6 amps. This is a very large current. A current this large would destroy your circuit board.

It is important to explain the importance for voltage

because LEDs have such a low resistance that if they are connected directly to the microcontroller, the current flow will damage the microcontroller. Microcontrollers typically can deliver up to 20 milliamps (mA) of current. In the example above, the current (6 amps) was 300 times this maximum.

As current starts to flow through an LED, the LED quickly warms up. As it does, its resistance drops, which allows more current to flow. In a powered circuit, the resistance becomes too low to operate safely. So in hooking up an LED to your circuit board, you need to put a resistor (an electronic component that reduces the flow of electricity) in series with it. That is, the connection needs to go from a microcontroller pin to a resistor, then to the LED, and finally to the ground (Vss). (Since the resistor controls the current flow throughout the circuit, it doesn't matter if it is in front of the LED or behind it. In either position, it will limit the current.)

Resistors come in many different values, and you need to select the right one. Using Ohm's law, you can calculate how much resistance the circuit needs. The current through the microcontroller must be less than 20 mA. Since the voltage supplied is 6, the minimum resistance will be:

$$R = V/I$$
$$= 6 \text{ volts}/0.020 \text{ amps} = 300 \text{ ohms}$$

You need a resistor that has a value greater than 300 ohms. If you use one that is much larger, say 10,000 ohms, the current through the LED will be quite small, and the LED will barely light up. A reasonable value for the resistor in our circuit is 470 to 1,000 ohms.

Use the breadboard to connect an LED and resistor (Figure 6.2). Make sure the long leg of the LED is either connected to the microcontroller pin or to the resistor, which

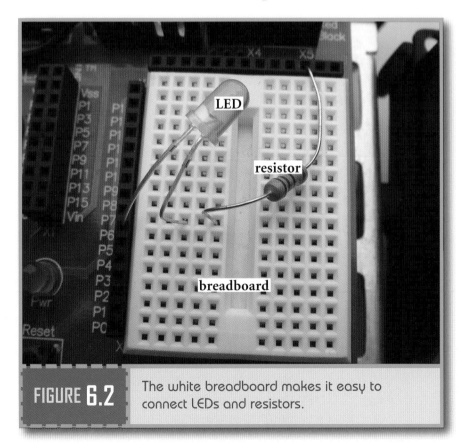

FIGURE **6.2** The white breadboard makes it easy to connect LEDs and resistors.

is then connected to the microcontroller pin. The other leg of the LED (or the resistor, if it follows the LED) connects to a Vss pin, which is at 0 volts or system ground.

Light an LED

Now write a program to control the LED. You can turn on the voltage at a pin just like a switch. "On" delivers +5 volts and "off" delivers 0 volts. In Parallax Basic, the commands that operate like a switch are "`high`" and "`low`."

If the LED/resistor circuit is connected to pin 6, the Parallax code would look like this:

```
high 6
pause 500
low 6
```

This code turns on the LED for half a second and then turns it off.

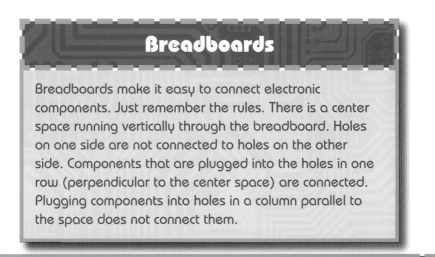

Breadboards

Breadboards make it easy to connect electronic components. Just remember the rules. There is a center space running vertically through the breadboard. Holes on one side are not connected to holes on the other side. Components that are plugged into the holes in one row (perpendicular to the center space) are connected. Plugging components into holes in a column parallel to the space does not connect them.

Flash an LED

Write a program that will repeatedly flash the LED on and off.

1. Wire an LED into the Parallax breadboard (see Figure 6.2 again). Wire the longer leg of the LED into the slot of an unused pin and the other leg into a hole in the breadboard. Make sure this hole is in a row that has no other components connected to the hole.

2. In an adjacent hole in the same breadboard row, insert one leg of a 470-ohm resistor. Insert the other leg of the resistor into one of the Vss slots. Now the LED is wired and ready to go.

3. Remember how you controlled the servo motors? You used a loop program that ran for a number of times, which you specified in a "`for x = ...`" statement. Use a loop program to turn the LED on and off. Remember that

Things you will need

- computer
- microprocessor
- LED
- resistor
- wire
- breadboard
- serial cable or USB connection

the code for powering an LED is "`high ____`", where you fill in the pin number that is connected to the LED.

In the example above, the pause command between turning the LED on and off specified that the pause was 500 milliseconds. The period does not need to be fixed; it can be variable. If the LED were in the slot of pin 6, the program could say

```
high 6
pause x
low 6
pause x
```

A program in your robot can turn LEDs on and off.

If you used this code in a loop, you could flash the LED on and off at a rate that varies according to the value of x.

If x is too small, the flash will be on for such a short time period, you won't be able to detect it. You could introduce a second variable, y, and make `y = 100*x`, and `pause y`. Then as the loop program gets to higher values of x, the LED will stay on for 100 times the value of x.

Variable Pulse Lengths

1. Introduce a second variable, y, and write an equation that specifies the value of y based on the value of x. Do you want the LED on for the same length of time as it is off? Or do you want to these two time periods to be different?

2. How else could you vary the time periods? What other equations for the variable y could you make? Look in the reference manual or online documentation to see what mathematical operators are available and how to use them.

LEDs can help you understand what is happening inside the microcontroller. A problem common with robots is that the batteries lose charge without you knowing. As the voltage drops below the threshold acceptable by the microcontroller, it will "brown out" or shut down. Once that happens, the

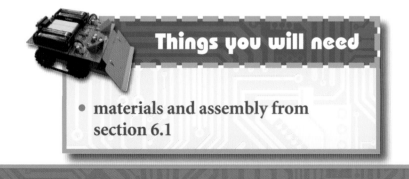

Things you will need

- materials and assembly from section 6.1

batteries quickly rebound. The voltage they can deliver can bounce back up above the threshold. The microprocessor now "sees" the acceptable voltage and starts running the resident program, starting from the first line. The robot starts running its program, stops, and goes back to the start of the program. This can happen over and over without your realizing that the problem is low batteries.

You can use an LED on your robot to alert you to low batteries. Have the LED flash on and off in a distinctive pattern at the start of each program you write. If in the middle of running a program you notice the distinctive flashing of the LED and odd behavior of your robot, you will know that the batteries are low, and it's time to replace them.

Control Lights with Cricket

You can operate an incandescent bulb with Cricket. The lightbulb should be rated for 6–9 volts and up to 100 milliamps. Wire it into any of the four motor outputs.

You could also use an LED. If you do this, wire it in series with a resistor (470 ohm). With either type of light, use the Cricket DF3 wiring plug. Insert the plug into any unused motor output.

To control the light, address the output port (A, B, C, or

D), followed by a comma, and then the command "on." The command "off" turns power off. For example,

```
to lightup
A, on
wait 10
A, off
end
```

After typing this into the Cricket Logo Program window, click on Download. Then type the name of the program, lightup, in the Command Center and hit return. The light or LED connected to port A should illuminate for 1 second and then turn off.

You can also specify how long to leave the power on with a command:

```
A, onfor 8
```

This turns the power on to the A output port for 0.8 seconds.

You can power two of the output ports at the same time by specifying which ports you want turned on. To get both C and D on for 1 second, use the command:

```
CD, onfor 10
```

Light Up

Take two to four lights and wire them into the Super Cricket. Then write some creative code to control the several lights. Can you make them blink in interesting patterns?

The Super Cricket normally outputs less than full voltage to the four output ports. On a scale of 0 (no power) to 8 (full power), the Cricket normally supplies power at level 4. To change this output (useful for changing light intensity and motor speed), set the power level by adding this command line to your program:

```
setpower 6
```

This statement will raise the power level from its normal value of 4 and set it to level 6.

1. Change the power level in your program for controlling lights or LEDs. Try dimming the lights and getting them back up.

2. Record what level of power works best for the lights or LEDs.

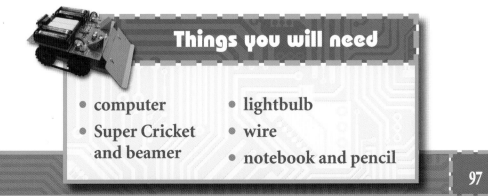

Things you will need

- computer
- Super Cricket and beamer
- lightbulb
- wire
- notebook and pencil

Add Touch Sensors

To be a real robot, a machine has to act independently of human control. That is, rather than following every instruction you give it, it should be receiving input from sensors, making choices, and taking action. This is the difference between a remote-control car and a robot.

Think about how hard it would be to write a program to move your robot through a maze. You would have to know the exact dimensions of the maze and then write a program to move and turn the robot at exactly the right position. That would have you working too hard and not taking advantage of what a robot does well. Instead, you can program the robot to find the walls and turn to avoid them. If the robot moves into a wall on the right side, you could program it to back up a few inches, and then turn left. If it moves into a wall directly in front of it, it could back up and few inches and turn to explore any new direction. Letting the robot choose options based on what it encounters takes advantage of the onboard microcontroller and uses the robot to its potential.

For the robot to know that it has hit a wall, it needs to convert the tactile sense into an electrical signal. That is, when it hits, a circuit has to close to alert the microcontroller. Since the device that controls circuits by opening and closing is a switch, you need to mount two switches on the robot. One should face the left front corner and the other should face the right front corner.

Microswitches work well for touch sensors (Figure 7.1). These devices have hundreds of other uses, such as detecting if your dishwasher door is open or closed. Because they are used in so many appliances, they are inexpensive and common. Electronic stores carry several to many different types. For your robot sensors, you will need two low-voltage switches or microswitches and some wire with clip leads.

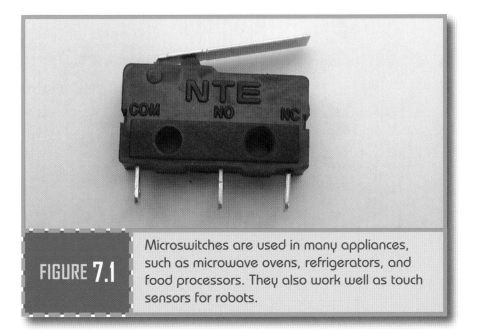

FIGURE 7.1 Microswitches are used in many appliances, such as microwave ovens, refrigerators, and food processors. They also work well as touch sensors for robots.

Test a Microswitch

Most microswitches give you two options. "Normally Open" (NO) means that the switch is open (not conducting electricity). "Normally Closed" (NC) means the switch is conducting electricity. When you press the lever, you open the switch. The third clip on the switch is "Common" (COM). It must be connected to operate either NO or NC.

1. Use some clip leads to connect a small motor and a microswitch in series. One wire will lead from a battery or battery case and go to the motor. The second wire will connect the other motor terminal to the COM clip on the microswitch. The third wire will connect the NO clip on the microswitch to the second terminal on the battery or case. Did anything happen when you made the connection?

Things you will need

- **microswitch**
- **battery or battery case**
- **wire with clip leads**
- **motor**

2. Depress the lever to see the motor spin. If nothing happens, try a different battery or check the wire leads. If they are functioning, try a different motor or a different switch to isolate the problem.

3. Switch the lead from NO to NC. Does the switch behave as you expected? You can use either mode (NO or NC) in your robot by adjusting the code you write. In the code below, use NO.

When you have experimented with the switches and understand how they work, figure out how you will connect them to the robot. They need a solid support so that they won't move when the robot bumps into an object. You will want to extend the sensor with a craft stick, dowel, or heavy straw. It has to extend far enough to cover the area in front of the robot (Figure 7.2). If the sensors do not close the switches completely, the robot could hit something without knowing it, and it would keep spinning its wheels and trying to go forward.

If the switch is closed (when the robot hits a wall), how will the microcontroller know? You need to build an electronic circuit that will allow the microcontroller to detect whether the switch is open or closed, and then you need to write the code telling the microcontroller what to do.

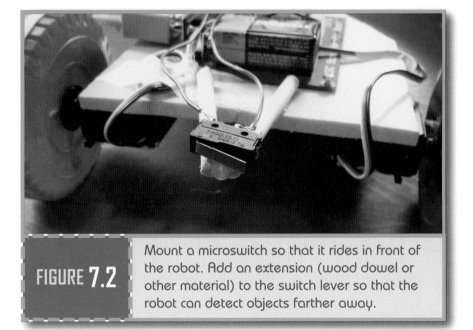

FIGURE 7.2 Mount a microswitch so that it rides in front of the robot. Add an extension (wood dowel or other material) to the switch lever so that the robot can detect objects farther away.

Microcontrollers, like all computers, operate on binary systems. Switches are "on" or "off." In small robots, "on" means that the voltage is 5V, and "off" means the voltage is 0V. To use a switch, you need a circuit that helps the microcontroller detect either 5V or 0V.

Building the Switch Circuit

You will need two switches and two resistors for each switch. The resistors should be 10,000 ohms and 220 ohms.

This is a "pull-down" circuit. When the Normally Open switch is closed, it "pulls down" the voltage sensed by the pin. The pin senses 0V. Figure 7.3 shows a circuit diagram.

When the switch is open (as shown), the pin detects 5V. The current through the pin is tiny because the circuit has a total of 10,220 ohms of resistance. To calculate the current, use Ohm's law:

I = V/R

I = 5/10,220

I = .00049 amp, or less than 0.5 mA. (The maximum safe current to flow to a microcontroller is 20 mA, which is 40 times the current that this circuit allows. Thus the microcontroller is safe. Although the **current flow** is tiny, the voltage is still 5V. The digital micro-controller reads this as a 1, or "on.")

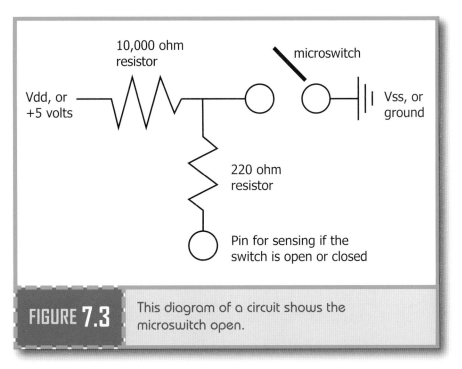

FIGURE 7.3   This diagram of a circuit shows the microswitch open.

What happens when the switch is closed? Current passes through the switch to Vss or ground, which has a voltage value of zero. Closing the switch puts the circuit at zero volts. The pin registers this as 0, or "off."

To make this circuit, start at an empty row in the breadboard. Three wires (from both resistors and from one side of the switch) connect to each other at the center of the circuit diagram above, so they will all plug into the empty row you choose. By putting them in a row (not a column), you connect them all with each other. The other end of the 10,000-ohm resistor gets inserted into a Vdd connector (Vdd provides +5V). The other end of the 220-ohm resistor is inserted into the slot for the pin you are going to use for the first switch. The other side of the switch gets connected to ground, or Vss.

Now you need a small program to test the switch. Here is where LEDs are again helpful. Write a program to turn on an LED when the switch is closed. First, wire an LED. Insert the long leg of the LED into the input/output pin #9. Insert the short leg into any slot in an unused row of the white breadboard. Insert one leg of a resistor (470 ohms) into another slot in the same row and the other leg into Vss. Now, you're ready to write the program.

Type this into your computer	Meaning of command
`'Program Switch Test`	Use the comment line to remind us what the program is about.
`start:`	"`Start`" is a label or address that can be referenced later in the program.
`if (in7 = 0) then light`	Chose pin 7 as the switch input pin. "`In`" tells the microprocessor that pin 7 is an input (not an output) pin. If pin 7 detects zero volts, it will go to the label that follows "`then`," which is "`light`".
`pause 50`	If the voltage isn't zero, go to the next line, which is pause 50 milliseconds.
`goto start`	Go back to the label "`start`".
`light:`	"`Light:`" is a label or address.
`high 9`	Turn pin 9 high (+5V) to light an LED connected (through a resistor) to this pin.
`pause 100`	Keep the LED on by pausing 100 milliseconds.
`low 9`	Turn the LED off.
`goto start`	Go back to the label "`start`".
`end`	End of the program.

What will this program do? It will operate indefinitely or until the battery runs out or you turn off the robot. It looks to see if the switch is depressed. If it is, then it lights the LED for 1/10 of a second. Then it turns the LED off and again looks to see if the switch is open or closed.

Build and Program a Switch Circuit

1. Connect the components on a breadboard, connect them to the circuit board, and copy the program above into your computer. Note that the program calls for the switch to be connected to pin 7 and the LED to pin 9. You can use any unused pins (not any that power servos or other LEDs) you want, but make sure that you change the pin numbers in the code to reflect the pins that the components are connected to. Remember, too, that the LED requires a resistor in series with it so that it won't draw current that will damage the microcontroller.

3. Check the wiring again, and then download the program to your robot to test the circuit. Does the LED come on?

4. Try a longer pause or have the LED flash on and off while the switch is closed.

Things you will need

- computer
- breadboard
- circuit board
- microswitches
- wire
- LED
- resistors
- serial cable or USB connection

Now that you can build and program a switch, add touch sensors to your robot.

Add Touch Sensors

7.3

COOL!

Now that you can build and program a switch, add touch sensors to your robot.

1. Mount two touch sensors to the front of your robot. You can glue them to the robot platform or attach them to a dowel or other material so that they project in front of the robot to opposite sides.

2. Wire the switches to the circuit board.

3. Test them using one or two LEDs as you did in section 7.2. When both switches work, you're ready to program your robot to navigate autonomously.

Write Code for Autonomous Navigation

What do you want the robot to do if the left sensor encounters a solid object? What do you want it to do if both sensors bump into something?

Things you will need

- computer
- mobile robot
- microswitches
- resistors
- wire
- LED
- dowels or other materials to hold microswitches
- serial cables or USB connection

Place your robot with its touch sensors in the position it would be if it just bumped into a wall on the left. Get the robot close enough so that the touch sensor is depressed. (The robot does not need to be powered now. Save your batteries!) Assume that the robot stopped in this position. What do you want it to do now?

Turning is probably out of the question. The robot is probably so close to the wall that it can't turn. First you need to have it back up. How far? Far enough so that the sensor won't hit the wall as it is turning. Look at your notes to decide how far (how many loops in a "`for x = 1 to . . .`" code) you need the robot to go. If you've forgotten the arguments for the "pulsout" command that will move the robot in reverse, look at your notes for section 5.3. That's why you took the time to record this data.

After the robot backs up far enough, what should it do? If it hits a wall on the left (the left sensor pin detects 0V), it probably needs to turn right. How far right do you want it to turn? A full 90-degree turn? Half a turn (45 degrees)? How many loops and what code will you need?

After the robot backs up and makes a turn, how far should it go before checking the touch sensors? Do you want it to check the sensors after every step? That would be the safest, but slowest, approach.

Here's a good programming strategy:

Declare any variables needed in the program.

Provide a label for the program to come back to: start.

Check both switches: if (in7 and in8 = 0) then reversedirections. (This directs the microprocessor to go to a label called "reversedirections." This label would provide code to have the robot back up and then turn 180 degrees and start anew.)

If only one is touching, check each one individually with "if" statements. If one switch is depressed, back up and turn away from that side. If the first switch isn't depressed, then check the second switch with another "if" statement, using the pin connected to the second switch.

If neither switch is touching, then step forward (go to a label marked "forward"). So the robot checks the switches.

Idea for a Science Fair Project

In your pile of components taken out of old appliances (from section 2.1), you might find some switches. You could also look in electronics stores for switches used in home alarms or audio equipment. Could you create your own switch? For a science fair project, you could test a variety of switches to see which ones work best on your mobile robot.

Navigate a Maze

1. Set up a maze to see if your programmed robot can get through (Figure 7.4). Use cardboard boxes, heavy books, and other flat objects for walls. Make the walls perpendicular to each other and higher than the touch sensors on your robot. Keep the path openings about 3 to 4 times as wide as the robot is.

2. Write the code to navigate a maze. Tackle the problem in pieces. You have written the code for switches, and you have written codes for turns and going forward and backward. Now put each piece in place and test it. Write the code for one switch and test it. Did the robot turn when you depressed this sensor? If not, solve this problem before making the code more complex.

3. When you have both switches working and the robot responding to the switches being closed, race your robot through the maze.

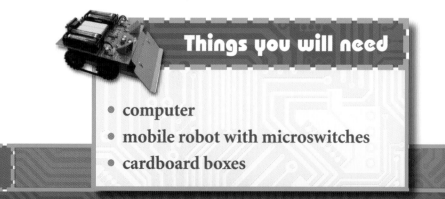

Things you will need

- computer
- mobile robot with microswitches
- cardboard boxes

FIGURE 7.4 Use cardboard boxes and walls to create a maze for your robot to find its way through.

Ideas for a Science Fair Project

- A measure of a robot's success in running a maze would be to average five or more trials through a maze. You could compare this average time to the same robot when it uses infrared sensors instead of touch sensors to navigate the maze. If you found a significant difference between the two average times, you could suggest a reason for the difference or ways to improve the times.

- You could also compare different operating programs (software) for the robot. Which one made the robot operate more effectively or faster? Does the robot move forward three pulses before checking sensors? Or does it check the sensors at each step?

- What geometry of a maze is difficult for a robot to exit? What geometry is easy? Different size openings, different angles between walls, and different wall heights can all contribute to a robot's success or failure. Can you measure these so that you understand which maze dimensions work well and which do not?

- Compete with other robot builders or with yourself to record the fastest run through a maze. Run the maze, then adjust the code to make the robot get through the maze more quickly. You could have it take several steps forward before checking the sensors. Or, you could change how far it turns to the side or how far it backs up when it runs into a wall. Save the code you write and record how fast the robot completes the maze with each code.

You can make your own switch assemblies by wiring a microswitch or other switch to two wires that connect to a plug that fits into the sensor ports. You can get the plugs from Gleason Research, or you can purchase switch kits that you assemble. In a program, you identify a switch by typing "`switchA`". This identifies the switch plugged into port A. Use "`waituntil [switchA]`" to control a motor or sound by closing the switch in port A.

1. Connect a switch to sensor port A and write a program that beeps when you close the switch (Figure 7.5). Type the following code into the Cricket Logo Program window, download it, and run it.

```
to switchsound
beep
wait 10
loop [waituntil [switchA] beep]
end
```

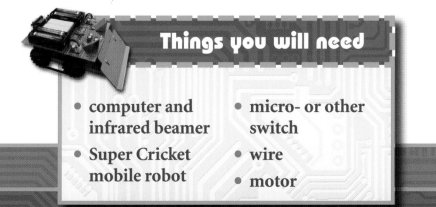

Things you will need

- **computer and infrared beamer**
- **Super Cricket mobile robot**
- **micro- or other switch**
- **wire**
- **motor**

113

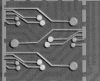

FIGURE **7.5**
A push button serves as the switch or sensor to sound a beep on a Cricket.

The "loop" command keeps checking to see if the switch is closed. When it is, it executes the command following [switchA], which is "beep." However, you could use another command, for example a servo or motor command following [switchA].

2. What happens if you hold the switch closed? Record the program and the results in your experiment notebook.

3. Another way to get the same result is to use an "if" command. Enter this code and try it:

```
to switchsound
beep
wait 10
loop [if switchA [beep]]
end
```

4. What happens if you keep the switch closed? Record this program and your results in your experiment notebook. Think of other uses of the commands "loop," "if," and "waituntil."

5. To turn on a motor with a push-button switch, connect a motor to motor port B and the push button to sensor port A. Motor ports and sensor ports are not the same. Look at the Super Cricket to see them clearly marked. Then try this code:

```
to motor
beep
loop [if switchA [B, onfor 33]]
end
```

Once you have downloaded and run this program, the Super Cricket will beep once and then start a loop, looking at the sensor in port A. When you depress the switch, the motor at B will turn on for 33 time units, or 3.3 seconds.

6. Connect a switch to one of the sensor ports and try using

FIGURE **7.6** Pushing the button starts the program that turns the motor on and off.

it to beep and to turn a motor on and off (Figure 7.6). If you don't have a switch handy, insert two wires (with stripped ends) into the outer holes of a 3-hole sensor plug and insert it into one of the sensor ports. Touching the two wires together will be your switch.

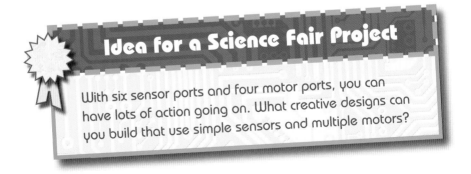

Idea for a Science Fair Project

With six sensor ports and four motor ports, you can have lots of action going on. What creative designs can you build that use simple sensors and multiple motors?

Use a Light Sensor

COOL!

A robot can respond to a wide variety of different sensors, provided that the electronic circuit is created to convert an action or condition to signals the robot can understand. In touch sensors, pushing the sensor shorted out the circuit, and the robot's microprocessor detected 0 volts on the sensor circuit. You can treat other sensors the same way: through their circuits, they supply either high voltage (5V) or low voltage (0V). Make sure that the voltages don't exceed 5, and that the currents are low enough that they don't damage the microcontroller.

The Super Cricket makes it easy to connect external sensors. Using the "sensor" command, the Cricket interprets the sensor signal (0 to 5V) as a number from 0 to 255. The Cricket can make a decision (using an "if" command) if the sensor has a value (light level, temperature, infrared radiation, etc.) that is high enough (or low enough) to trigger

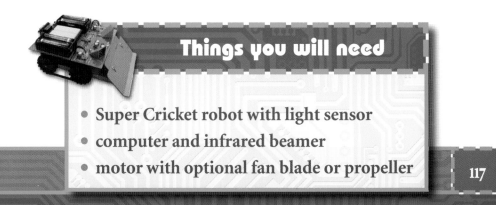

Things you will need

- **Super Cricket robot with light sensor**
- **computer and infrared beamer**
- **motor with optional fan blade or propeller**

some operation. For example, you could make a device that turns on a fan if the temperature gets too high. You would tell the Cricket what "too high" is by specifying a number between 0 and 255. You would determine that number by experimenting with a temperature probe.

More complex systems can be added that interpret data streams. For example, the signals coming from a television remote control (which are infrared coded pulses) can provide detailed information to the robot (Figure 7.7). With a TV remote-control unit, you can drive your robot like a remote-control car (which usually uses radio and not infra-red signals).

Robot suppliers offer a variety of sensors for temperature, humidity, light, infrared light, sounds, and touch. Infrared LEDs can send signals that bounce off objects, and the reflection can be detected by infrared receivers on robots (Figure 7.8). This is another way to have the robot avoid objects or to move toward objects.

Light sensors are photo-resistors, semiconductors whose resistance varies with the amount of light that hits them. The more light they are exposed to, the lower their resistance (Figure 7.9). Their resistance can be quite low in bright sunlight and very high (maybe 50,000 ohms) in darkness. A robot's

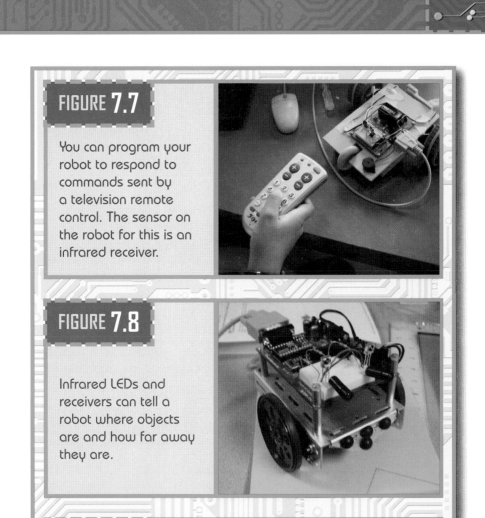

FIGURE 7.7

You can program your robot to respond to commands sent by a television remote control. The sensor on the robot for this is an infrared receiver.

FIGURE 7.8

Infrared LEDs and receivers can tell a robot where objects are and how far away they are.

FIGURE 7.9

A photo or light sensor is easily added to a Cricket.

microprocessor can distinguish the change in resistance. The change in resistance can trigger a switch to open or close.

The Super Cricket is well suited for using light and other sensors. You wire the photo-resistor into a plug, pushing the connecting wires into the outer two connections and inserting the plug into any of the six sensor sockets.

Because each photo-resistor will behave differently, you first need to determine the values the sensor delivers under different light levels. Say you want your robot to beep when light levels rise. You might want a light-activated burglar alarm, so when someone turns on the light in your room, your robot starts beeping. First you need to determine at which levels of light you want the beeping to start.

1. With the sensor inserted into the Super Cricket (sensor socket F), measure light levels. Type the following program into the Cricket Logo Program window:

```
to testsensor
beep
loop [send sensorF]
end
```

When you download and run this program, the Super Cricket will beep and then start displaying numerical values in the Cricket Monitor window. The loop command will keep sending the values measured at sensor socket F until you turn it off. Run this program and see what values show up in the Monitor window.

2. Move the sensor to different light conditions, or bring lights closer to the sensor to make the light level change.

Select a light level numerical value that will be the switching point. Note that brighter lights return lower values, so if you want the robot to beep when lights are bright, you'd use code similar to this:

```
to lightness
beep
loop [if sensorF < 50 [beep]]
end
```

This program beeps once to let you know that it has started and then continuously loops, testing the sensor. When lights are bright and the sensor sends back a reading less than 50, the robot will beep—and keep beeping.

3. To alert you to darkness, write code similar to this:

```
to darkness
beep
loop [if sensorF > 100 [beep]]
end
```

When the sensor detects low light levels and returns values greater than 100, the robot will beep.

4. Write a program that will turn on a small motor when

light levels are high. With a propeller or fan blade on the motor, you can set your fan (motor) to turn on when the sun rises and go off when the sun sets. Of course, don't leave it on too long or you will drain the batteries.

5. How else could you use a light sensor? Mess around with the sensor to see how it responds to different lights and light levels. Then come up with a new use for the it.

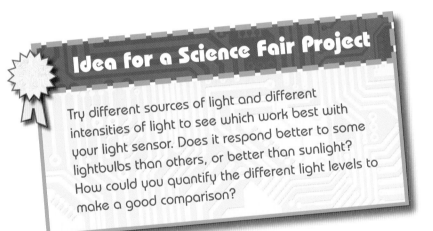

Idea for a Science Fair Project

Try different sources of light and different intensities of light to see which work best with your light sensor. Does it respond better to some lightbulbs than others, or better than sunlight? How could you quantify the different light levels to make a good comparison?

Appendix
Sources for Robot Components

There are several different robot systems available that will work for you. The three following systems are recommended:

Advanced Micro Circuits Corporation (http://world-educational-services.info/contact.html) sells PICAXE. Programming is in BASIC. PICAXE provides inexpensive components that work well for simple robots.

Gleason Research (http://gleasonresearch.com) sells Super Cricket, a popular system that is very different from the Parallax system. Super Cricket makes it easy to add a wide variety of sensors and motors. You don't have to create an additional electronic circuit for an interface between the sensors or motors and the circuit board.

Parallax (www.parallax.com) has several boards and microcontrollers, plus a variety of components. The Board of Education (Boe-Bot) kits and Homework Boards provide an inexpensive way for students to jump into robotics.

Glossary

breadboard—A plastic device that allows you to connect electronic components quickly and without the use of solder.

circuit board—A plastic sheet onto which electronics components are anchored and connected by solder.

diode—An electronic component that allows electrical current to flow in only one direction.

EEPROM—A memory chip that retains the data even when power is removed. The letters stand for Electrically Erasable Programmable Read-Only Memory.

ground—In robotics, ground is connected to the negative side of the power source or battery. In your home "ground" means zero voltage.

LED (light-emitting diode)—A diode that emits light when electric current flows through it.

linear actuator—A motor device that moves backward and forward in a line, unlike most motors, which move in a circular motion.

microcontroller (or MCU)—A small computer or microprocessor usually mounted on a circuit board.

microswitch—An electric switch used to turn on and off circuits and to indicate when doors (refrigerator doors, for example) are open.

Muscle Wire—Wire made of a combination of metals, or alloy, that returns to its original length and shape after being heated. Passing current through a muscle wire causes it to change length and shape, and on cooling (when the current is off) returns to its original length and shape.

Ohm's law—A basic law of electricity and electronics that relates the voltage in a circuit to the current and resistance (V = IR).

resistor—An electronics component that reduces the current in a circuit.

servo motor—A motor used in robotics to control the position of flaps, switches, and levers.

stepper motor—An electric motor that rotates in steps or small increments of a full rotation.

voltage—The electrical force between two points in an electrical circuit.

Further Reading

Books

Henderson, Harry. *Modern Robotics: Building Versatile Machines*. New York: Chelsea House Publishers, 2006.

Jones, David. *Mighty Robots: Mechanical Marvels that Fascinate and Frighten*. Toronto: Annick Press, 2005.

Thomas, Peggy. *Artificial Intelligence*. Farmington Hills, Mich.: Lucent Books, 2005.

VanVoorst, Jennifer Fretland. *Rise of the Thinking Machines: The Science of Robots*. Minneapolis, Minn.: Compass Point Books, 2008.

Internet Addresses

NASA. "NASA Robotics – Students: Inspiration." 2010.
<http://robotics.nasa.gov/students/students.php>

The Tech Museum of Innovation.
"Robotics: Sensing, Thinking, Acting." 2005.
<http://www.thetech.org/robotics/>

Index